Your Guide to Becoming a Qualified Salsa Teacher

Published by:

Thomas O'Flaherty

(Subconscious Whispers and www.spiritsalsa.com)

PO BOX 14854

BIRMINGHAM B18- 9EL

ISBN 978-0-9532429-2-4

ISBN-10:0953242927

ISBN-13:978.0953242924

Flat 45 Bismillah Building, Constitution Hill, B19 3LY, England.

Your Guide to Becoming a Qualified Salsa Teacher

SALSA

A teacher's guide covering everything from the origins of Salsa; different styles of salsa dancing, a 20 week learning syllabus of moves from Cuba, New York, LA and Colombia, teaching methods, learning styles and how to start your own salsa dance practice.

This book starts with my personal experience of salsa dance and explains the history of salsa from a worldwide historical view point. It traces England's influence on the roots of salsa dancing and the development of the UK salsa scene. This book is divided into practical guidance and theoretical exercises. The book will tell you about the different ways to teach salsa, the rules and regulations you must follow and how to set-up a salsa dance school. It shows you everything you need to set yourself up as a salsa dance teacher.

Written by Thomas O'Flaherty and Edited by Diana Sinclair.

Acknowledgements:

John Mullings for introducing me to salsa, Robert Charlemange for his guidance, Eddie the Salsa Freak, Fransisco Vasquez and Eddie Torres for being inspirational role models. To Maverick Logan and Annie Buzanne for their belief in me.

Your Guide to Becoming a Qualified Salsa Teacher

Contents

Your Guide to Becoming a Qualified Salsa Teacher

Your Guide to Becoming a Qualified Salsa Teacher

My Journey into Salsa

"When I hear music, I fear no danger.
I am invulnerable. I see no foe.
I am related to the earliest times, and the latest."
Thoreau, Journal, 1857

Since the age of nine I have loved dancing to reggae music, listening to Dennis Brown and Gregory Isaacs. From the age of fourteen I danced to hip-hop and then joined the Street Rock dance group. Aged twenty-four I did African dance with Kokuma dance company under the direction of Jackie Guy.

It was in 1995 that a friend of mine took me to a Latin dance club on Broad Street in Birmingham, UK, called Tramps. It was my 27th birthday and I saw who I now know to be DJ Maverick of Salsa Fabulous, dancing and playing salsa music. It was totally foreign to me but I went onto more parties and was dragged onto the dance floor to dance the mambo by a lady called Karen who taught me my very first salsa step at Los Amigos, a Latino restaurant in Birmingham owned by Annie Buzanne. I had no feel for the music as far as salsa was concerned. I realized that the rhythm was addictive and I kept coming back for more. I decided to learn the dance properly and took a few classes at the Custard Factory with Mauricio Reys of Latin Motion.

Your Guide to Becoming a Qualified Salsa Teacher

When I went to salsa clubs very few girls would dance with me because I had little technique and I would randomly spin and dip my dance partners without leading them properly, I would also make them look bad because my dancing was chaotic. I was more concerned with impressing my friends rather than dancing properly. Eventually the salsa rhythms seeped into my soul and I became a good salsa dancer. I found a hobby where I could meet friends and release tension at the end of a hard week of stressful work.

Salsa music has the unique ability to create feelings of euphoria, relaxation and spiritual enlightenment. It gave me a magical feeling that I never experienced with any other type of music. It was after about one year of salsa dancing at XLs night club in Birmingham run by Maverick Logan that dancers from London would visit and dance a different style based on the new American LA style which is based on the cross body lead. The visiting London dancers were Robert Charlemagne, Special T and Dean Maynard. They introduced me to a dance style called LA style. It was totally different to what I knew which was a mixture of Cuban, Colombian and Cumbian styles.

In 1997 I went to the University of Coventry and studied French and Spanish with linguistics. In my spare time, at student parties, I always showed off my dance skills and people would ask me to show them how to dance. It got to the point where I was asked to put on a class. I never had any desire to teach, I simply did it because I was asked so often. My first class was attended by twenty-five people and luckily everyone said they enjoyed the class even though I had no teaching qualifications or real technique. However, the students enjoyed the classes because I taught in a relaxed way and focused on them having fun.

In the late 90s I really threw myself into salsa competitions and I entered 10 salsa competitions and won 5 of them. I travelled to Holland for the European Salsa Championships, and attained a second round placing against truly rhythmic and original dancer from all over the world. It was very exciting and filmed on Dutch Television.

The competitions I entered abroad opened my eyes to how far behind the UK was in comparison to the rest of Europe and the world. I went to Spain in 1999 and met Cubans who taught me Cuban style salsa which seemed much more advanced and rhythmical than which I had learned in the UK. With the knowledge gained from the Cubans I made choreographies for shows in France, Spain and the UK.

When I returned to Birmingham in 2000 I decided to learn how to teach dance with professional training. I did a diploma in dance, incorporating Salsa, Puerto Rican salsa on to mambo, cha cha cha and merengue with the UKA. I was the first non-ballroom salsa instructor to qualify to teach salsa in the UK outside of London.

Following three years of qualified teaching I developed a course on how to teach Caribbean and Latin dance funded by United Millennium Awards. The course covered Cuban, Brazilian, Dominican dances, music and cultural history. This course took my direction from entering salsa competitions to community workshops for people on low incomes and for educational projects.

Your Guide to Becoming a Qualified Salsa Teacher

The Caribbean and Latin dance project (2003) was a project I designed to train people on how to teach dance. The project focused on helping students and people on low income to develop into dance teachers. This is when I first found my calling. It gave me a sense of purpose to teach dance and to share my passion, knowledge and experience. It is also the reason why I want to write this book on Your Guide to Becoming a Qualified Salsa Teacher.

Chapter 1

In this chapter you learn about:

- the definitions of salsa

- salsa history in the UK and worldwide

Your Guide to Becoming a Qualified Salsa Teacher

WHAT IS SALSA?

"Afro Hispanic Caribbean song and dance form rooted in the Cuban son that is today an internationalised form no longer associated with any one country"
p 510, The Garland Handbook of Latin American Music, 2nd ed, Dale A, Olsen and Daniel El. Sheehny. Routledge New York, 2008

"Salsa is the folklore of the city, not of one city but of all cities of Latin America"
Ruben Blades- Salsa, DVD, A Jeremy Marre Documentary, Harcourt Films 1979.

*"One of the most expressive, passionate and creative social dances in the world"*Thomas O'Flaherty.

The music:

Salsa music is a definition created by Izzy Sanabria to cover all the Latin Caribbean music that was played by Fania All Stars, a Latin super group composed of Cubans, Puerto Ricans and Dominicans during the 60's and 70's. Like Jazz, salsa has become an abstract term which implies energy, excitement and hot spice as in its name sake, a hot pepper sauce, p8 (S. Steward, Salsa 1999).

Definition:

 A mixture of Cuban and Puerto Rican based rhythms developed in New York by Fania All Stars.

A marketing term for Latin American music.

Jazz mixed with Caribbean and South American music.

A mixture of Spanish and African music.

"The vertical expression of the horizontal desire!"

A final word: The one element that unifies Latin and Caribbean music in rhythm is the clave. The clave rhythm is produced by two wooden sticks (claves) which are about 7 inches long to create a percussive sound to start the beginning of a rhythm.

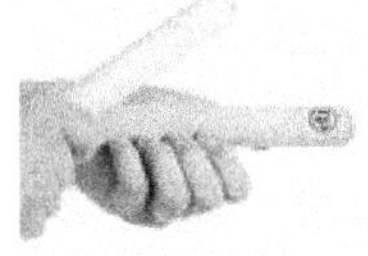

The Dance:

Salsa music is a mixture of rhythms and the dance is also be a mixture of dance styles to follow those rhythms! Depending on which definition you accept that will define the dance style of salsa you teach.

Your Guide to Becoming a Qualified Salsa Teacher

A List Of Latin And Caribbean Dances Used In Salsa:

Mambo Cubano and Mambo Americano,

pachanga,

bolero,

conga de comparsa,

danzon,

son,

rumba and its three variations: guaguanco, colombia, yambu,

cha cha cha,

zapateo - a flamenco derived folk dance once popular throughout Cuba.

Pilon - developed around cutting sugar cane.

Cumbia - a side step shuffle from Columbia.

"The essence of a thing is in its origin" Saul Kripke

The History of Salsa: A World Wide Historical View:

Through war, colonisation and the fusion of European and African
cultures in the Caribbean, salsa dance and music developed. Following
is a brief explanation of how dance that originated with English Country
dance migrated across Europe and finally arrived in the Caribbean. The
roots go even further back than England because English Morris dancing
is said to be an import of Spain which the Spanish adopted from the
Moors (Moorish, Morescos of Muslim Arabia) who ruled Spain for almost
800 years.

Your Guide to Becoming a Qualified Salsa Teacher

"The morris or Moorish dance was first brought in England as I take it, in Edward III time when John of Gaunt returned from Spain"

p21 History of the Morris Dance, A look at Morris Dancing from its earliest days until 1850. Dance Books, Alton Hampshire 2005. John Gaunt.

England's claim to the French crown by Edward III caused the 100 years war between France and England from 1337. English country dancing was then adapted by French royalty.

The French royals assimilated these English country dances and modified them into Contre danse. Later in the 18th c. Louis XIV took the Spanish crown and caused the War of Spanish succession and exported the French Contre danse which the Spanish adapted into Contra danza (Country dance).

The French ruled the Spanish for many years causing more wars and revolutions. The French Revolution, during the reign of Louis XVI used dance to control his Royal courtiers by forcing them to come to Versailles. He made them learn dance routines which were designed for two reasons: first, to ensure hierarchy between rulers and servants and secondly, to draw the power base where he could control it, in Versailles. So he made it difficult for anyone to overthrow him, although they eventually did.

During the Napoleonic war, Napoleon installed his brother Joseph as a puppet king in Spain causing the peninsular war 1808. During these wars the French installed their ways of living and cultural activities, one of which being dances in royal circles. The French Revolution and Napoleonic war were also taking place in the Caribbean, which at the time was still a colony of European powers consisting of the English, Spanish, French and the Dutch. The Spanish colonized Haiti but the French overthrew the Spanish and colonized the west side of the Island (now Haiti) of Hispaniola which is shared with the Dominican Republic.

At the beginning of the French Revolution, African slaves lead by Toussaint Breda) Louverture, revolted against their masters and ruled independently for almost 21 years until 1843. During this time the slaves imitated their ex-masters royal court dances such as Contra Danza which developed into Danzon. When the Spanish regained their colony, many of the ex French slaves fled to the neighbouring Caribbean island of Cuba, where they landed on the coast of Santiago.

From the 14th c. in England to 19th c. in Cuba, English country dancing has migrated, adapted and mixed with African dances and transformed into Cuban folk dances. Listed below are some styles of Cuban folk dance.

Cuban folk dances:
Son
Rumba :- Columbia, Guaguanco and Yambu
Pachanga

Your Guide to Becoming a Qualified Salsa Teacher

Palo de conga de comparsa

Guaracha

Cha cha cha

Danzon, Habanera and bolero

Mambo

Afro dance

Orishas - lecumi African spiritual deities.

Cuban music and dance flourished from the influences of the French and Spanish courts, Romany gypsy harmonies and African rhythms. The free slaves, now servants or indentured servants were allowed to practice their religions and were allowed to celebrate Christianity. Therefore they combined their African deities with Christian saints and developed a religion called Santeria. In Cuba all the Christian saints are paired with Yoruban (African) spirits. So the Cubans have an opportunity to retain their African historical roots, "in consultation with the church, the Spanish government established cabildos (chapter houses or naciones) which were founded on ethnic lines". p21 (S Steward, Salsa 1999)

Between the 18th and 20th centuries Cuba changed colonial hands from Spain to America. In the 20th century America went through the depression and this caused drastic cut backs in food and luxuries such as alcohol. Alcohol was banned in the late 1920s and this prohibition lead to white Americans flocking to the Caribbean for cheap alcohol from their nearest rum producing island, Cuba. The Hispanic (Spanish speaking people) Americans from Cuba and Puerto Rico were not rich enough to travel so easily and they distilled their own rum illegally having small homemade parties. These parties developed into community groups and social clubs which we will refer back to later in this book. The Americans who went to Cuba started businesses in gambling, prostitution and set up hotels and casinos. Many of these Americans were gangsters, Al Capone and Lucky Luciano were involved in Cuban stocks and companies. Al Capone's house still stands in Varadero. The gangsters had many areas of business that flourished outside of America which included the sale of alcohol and gambling in casinos. Americans went to Cuba, got drunk and enjoyed the social scene which included the entertainment from the ballrooms and street dancing of the Cubans. With reference to salsa today: there are many dance performances where the dancer will wear a pin striped suit and gangster hat to refer to the American Jazz influences during prohibition. Americans were fascinated by the exotic dancing and wild rhythms Cubans exhibited.

The Americans imitated these dances and rhythms and took them back to America after prohibition. At that time any type of exotic dancing was looked down upon by Western society. This made it even more attractive to those who enjoy forbidden fruit! The dances from Cuba were too syncopated for western ears so the rhythms were simplified, but in their simplification they were incorrectly labelled. The Americans confused rumba for mambo and taught all the movements in a very sanitised way with little hip movement or syncopation. America also mixed Cuban music with Jazz giving it a more contemporary sound. Genres such as son and danzon developed in Cuba but once exported to America developed into a new style of mambo and cha cha cha. New forms of Latin jazz emerged in the 60s such as bebop. In the 60s rock and roll took over the popularity of Latin jazz and this genre started to die out. Latin dances in New York ballroom were closing down. Band orchestra leaders such as Machito and Tito Puente were losing their appeal.

This is when a marketing genius came to reinvent the wheel with some marketing spin. Izzy Sanabria was an MC but more importantly the promoter of the most famous Latin group of the time, the Fania All Stars. Izzy needed to package and label the product of Latin music from the Caribbean before it died out. Izzy used the term salsa as a catchall umbrella term for all the Latin rhythms to increase Fania All Stars' marketing appeal. This definition was fine at the time because it ensured the survival of Latin Caribbean music from Cuba and Puerto Rico. Since the late 90s the definition started to create problems for musicians because so many record labels described their music as salsa when it had no relation to the music that the Fania All Stars intended to describe. Even the lead singer of Fania All-Stars, who was widely acknowledged as the Queen of salsa: Celia Cruz, herself said there was no such thing as salsa, and that there was only specific rhythms like guaracha, mambo, rumba, cha cha danzon, son etc. The great Latin band leader, widely acknowledged as the King of Mambo, Tito Puento himself acknowledged that he plays mambo and other rhythms but there is no actual rhythm called salsa. Izzy Sanabria used the description to sell records of Fania All Stars and their music used Spanish words with Cuban, Puerto Rican and Dominican rhythms which were mainly played in 4/4 time but sometimes 2/4 time signatures such as merengue.

The definition of salsa music has now become a victim of its own success because musical rhythms from such countries as Argentina, Brazil and Jamaica are being mixed with Latin instrumentation into their music and called it salsa. So we end up with a constantly changing hybrid of music which almost has no similarity to what was intended back in the 70s when the term was first used by Izzy Sanabrias Fania All Stars.

Salsa history in the UK

In the 80s, and early 90s in the UK salsa would be danced by doing basic steps composed of the side step, a back step, an open step, or 3 steps followed by tap. Teachers from South America and the Caribbean island of Cuba would teach in London. Homero Gonzalez from Cuba was one of the first established salsa teachers in London.

The late 90s bought about change in the way salsa was danced. Americans came over and danced salsa with the forward and back mambo step which incorporated the cross body lead and lots of turns.

A lady called Edie, a.k.a. Edie the Salsa Freak distributed videos of her performances in this style which was then known as LA style. She then sold videos and DVDs worldwide based on the LA style of salsa. The UK followed her teaching until the late 1990s and early 2000 when a gentleman called Eddie Torres came and performed shows in the New York mambo salsa. He trained teachers and developed what the author knows as the Eddie Torres technique Salsa Night Club Style.

Eddie Torres in his videos and DVDs acknowledges the roots of his movement and style as Cuban, in volumes 1 and 2. Eddie Torres was the pioneer for salsa mambo style in the UK and all over the world. Unfortunately some people have tried to segregate the roots of what he taught from Cuban style and there are camps of dancers who will not dance with each other because they believe that their styles are ultimately too different or superior. Eddie Torres also taught his style to be danced on the second beat of the bar. He also used different techniques for leaders preparing the followers' turns. Some people interpreted that the LA style taught by Eddie the Freak must also be taught the same way as Edie Torres and confusion reigned.

Some people assumed the style in the UK, pre Eddie Torres was an incorrect style, although it could be argued that the American style was also an incorrect version of Cuban style. This led to many UK teachers squabbling over who was a good teacher and who was not based on the style they taught. Apart from the confusion and resentment this created, it also leads to a fracturing of the salsa scene in the UK. If you have studied Eddie's videos and taken his classes you will see and understand that this was never his intention. You will also notice that his style and teaching are strongly influenced by Cuban dance styles of son and rumba.

The most influential dancer who came before Eddie Torres is Cuban Pete (Pedro Aquilar), who was not Cuban at all but Puerto Rican and he danced New York mambo on 2, to the clave rhythm. He is reported to have created 100 steps which are used in salsa dancing today including the cross body lead. Songs have been written about him and films made about his life in New York. The city of New York have proclaimed June 14th Cuban Pete day. He was around New York in the 40's dancing mambo which is what we now call salsa. This reference to Cuban Pete can be read on the salsa power website:

http://www.salsapower.com/cubanpete/legend/ and the video the spirit moves. Reference: The Spirit Moves by Mura Dehn.

Your Guide to Becoming a Qualified Salsa Teacher

Chapter 2

In this chapter you learn about:

- theories on teaching

- a 20 week program covering:

- 68 salsa moves from Cuban, North American and Colombia

- the Clave rhythm and the Danzon

Your Guide to Becoming a Qualified Salsa Teacher

"What matters is not what any individual thinks but what is true, a teacher who does not equip their pupils with the rudimentary tools to discover this, is substituting indoctrination for teaching"

1996 Ethics and Education THEORIES

The Different Styles of Salsa

There are many styles of salsa that can be danced to salsa music which as mentioned in the definition is a mix a Latin and Caribbean rhythms. In this section of the book you will find a large list of salsa moves; 68 from Cuba, Los Angeles and New York in addition to moves from Colombia. You should use this list as a learning resource. It is suggested that you learn 4 moves per week in order to complete the list within 20 weeks. Type the name of the moves into www.spiritsalsa.com search box. When you have found the video, save it to your video favourites so that you can refer to it again after you have copied and practised it. The moves have been segmented into 4 moves per week in their respective categories.

Whether you can dance Cuban style, Colombian style, American LA style or American New York style there will always be sub variations of these.

Your Guide to Becoming a Qualified Salsa Teacher

Of the many derivative styles based on these styles such as Paris style, Porto Rican style or even London style! Whichever style you choose to teach you will always have to refer to its origin to establish fundamental moves and steps which will be at its essence and make it salsa. The original style of salsa is Cuban and this is where we will start.

Cuban Style:

A couple dance where the woman dances around the man, where all the movements are circular. The couple can also dance in a large circle with other couples. This is called the Rueda de Casino, thus named, because it originated in a Casino in Cuba. The couples change partners in response to a person's call to perform the following move. This goes all the way back to English country dancing; many of the moves are similar to the original ones from the 17th century.

The Cuban Salsa Style Developed From Cuban Folk Dances:

1 Son, developed from Spanish guitar and gypsy songs

2 Rumba- Columbia, Guaguanco and Yambu, Pachanga, developed from West African dance based around call and response and Spanish zapateo dances. The conga drum is used to express these rhythms. When the slaves from Africa came to the Caribbean, several tribes of the Yoruba, Abacua, the Dahomean and Congolese brought their rhythms. (Reference: Play Congas now by Richie Gatate-Garcia, p 10.)

3 Palo de conga de comparsa, West African dance

4 Guaracha, early predecessor of salsa with a quick melodic gallop

5 Cha cha cha, a syncopated step to interpret the music

6 Danzón, a developed form of Contra danza and English country dancing, which migrated to France and from Spain to the French

Caribbean and then to the Spanish Caribbean and ending up in Cuba. It is also connected to the Habanera, another Cuban dance.

7 Mambo, derived from the rhythms of danzon and called Nuevo ritmo or new rhythm, montuno section of a danzon.

8 Afro Cuban dance, Orishas = lucumi African spiritual deities. This dance and music is from the Yoruban tribe in West Africa and was preserved by the slaves and paired with the catholic religion.

To truly understand Cuban style, each of the above eight styles of dance themes must be studied. From this base of knowledge of Cuban folk dance will come a deep understanding of salsa moves, attitude and etiquette which is transferable to all styles of salsa worldwide. At the heart of the Cuban music and therefore the dance, is the clave rhythm which is the key to understanding Latin music. The next section will look at salsa music composition because without an understanding of the music the dance cannot be interpreted to any advanced level.

REVIEW:

1. Which style of Cuban dance first developed into salsa?
2. How many styles of Cuban dance were referred to?
3. Where did the Mambo originate from?

Your Guide to Becoming a Qualified Salsa Teacher

A List of 48 Cuban Rueda Moves:

"To teach well is to be a life long student"
Jonetta Betschcole, Conversations with Americas sister President 1993.

All these moves can be viewed on www.spiritsalsa.com/videos.htm at no
cost. You should study level 1 rueda moves to get a solid foundation of
most salsa moves.

Week 1

Level 1

Al Centro –to the centre
Para (Pa') arriba (y Muevete) -forward
Dile que no- tell her no
Guapea (or "No") beautify her

Week 2

Mirala - look at her
Dame (y otra) – give me one
Enchufla (or enchufe) –plug in,
Rompela -break her

Week 3

Enchufla doble –blow plug in twice
Castigala –punish her
Pelota / Pelota Doble –ball, double ball
Yogurt -

Your Guide to Becoming a Qualified Salsa Teacher

Week 4

Guaguanco -rumba

Adíos -goodbye

Prima -cousin

Enchufla Hombres al Centro blow men to the centre

Week 5

Rosa -rose

Paso Espanol -spanish step

Tarrito -cheat

Tarrito con Mentira –cheat but change your mind

Week 6

Daiqiri

Ni para tí ni para mi- neither for you nor for me

Level 2

Prima con la hermana -cousin with the sister

Dame Dos give me 2

Week 7

Festival de enchuflas festival of plug ins

Sígueme follow me

Pa' Abajo backwards

Dos con dos 2 with 2

Week 8

Enchufla con Vuelta plug in with turn

Siete 7

Vacílala show her off

Vacílala con dame show her off and change partners

Week 9

Abrazame hug me

Guarapo

Candado padlock

Candado Doble / Guaguanco double padlock

Week 10

Baila con migo dance with me

Sombrero hat

Peek-a-boo

Level 3

Setenta 70

Week 11

A la derecha (& Mujeres a la derecha) to the right and women to the right

Ochenta 80

A la izquierda (& Mujeres) to the left and women to the left

Una para Abajo one goes back

Week 12

Prima con hermana con la Tia (la Familia)cousin with sister and aunt, family,

Mauricio

Todos (a la derecha/izquierda)/ Cambio evrbody to the right, left

Pa'fuera/Pa'dentro (guapea,dame) outside, inside rueda

Week 13

Chocolate

Enchufla y Sacal plug her in and pull her out

American Salsa Styles: New York and LA.

The American salsa styles are based around the mambo step (different from the Cuban Mambo) and the cross body lead (based on the Cuban Dile que no). The Di le que no is the third move at level 1 of Cuban Rueda moves.

Here is a list of American LA and New York style salsa moves:

Level 1

Mambo

Cross body lead

Week 14

Right hand turn

Left hand turn

Level 2

Double left turn

Double right turn

Week 13

The copa

Your Guide to Becoming a Qualified Salsa Teacher

The hammerlock
Inside turn with the cross body lead
Outside turn with the cross body lead

Week 14

The travelling 360 cross body lead
The in and out
(The above moves are combined to create 100s of moves; they are all variations of the same basic salsa patterns).

Shines: A.K.A footwork

The hook step
The hook turn

Week 15

The swing step
The suzy q
The double front crosses
 The cord step

Week 16

Heel heel toe toe
V basic (mambo)

The LA style is normally danced on beat number 1. The New York style was danced according to the clave rhythm on beat number 2, now called on 2 salsa.

Your Guide to Becoming a Qualified Salsa Teacher

The Colombian salsa style is based on a mixture of Cuban rumba
Colombia, pachanga, boogaloo and the New York shines and jazzy
swing steps of the 1940s.
Pachanga

 1. Paso Basico basic step

 2. Basico Atras Con Patada Adelante: back step with forward tap

Week 17

 3. Basico Atras Con Giro De Cadera Y Tobillo Alto: back basic with hip
turn high ankles

 4. Basico Atras Con Giro De Cadera Y Punta Adelante: back basic with
turn of the hips

 5. Punta Continuas Con Giro De Cadera continuas: taps with turn of the
hips

6. Puntas Adelante Con Giro De Cadera: forward taps with turn of the
hips

Week 18

 7. Puntas Adelante Con Giro De Cadera Y Cruce: forward taps with turn
of the hips and cross

8. El Ciclon cyclone

9. Ciclon Continuo continuous cyclone

Boogaloo

1. Basico De Boogaloo basic boogaloo

Week 19

2. Basico Con Patada Cruzada basic cross tap. Patada Alta Con Cruce Por Delante high tap with behind cross

4. Micaela

5. La X: the cross

Week 20

6. Picapiedra Flint stone

Reference: http://www.worldsalsafederation.com/SyllabusStepLists.html

"Music sets up a certain vibration which unquestionably results in a physical reaction. Eventually the proper vibration for every person will be found and utilised" George Gershwin

Understanding the base of salsa music

The Clave

The importance of the clave rhythm is crucial in salsa so a detailed depiction of it will be provided. Each of the above mentioned dances are polyrhythmic meaning they have separate rhythms within rhythms. There are many clave rhythms and those used for salsa are the son clave 2/3 or 3/2 time signature, the rumba clave 3/2 signature or the afro Cuban 6/8 clave with 4/4 time signature.

3-2 Rumba clave

2-3 rumba clave

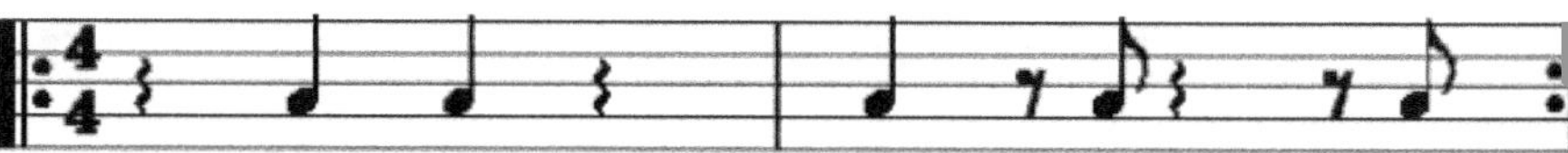

2-3 son clave

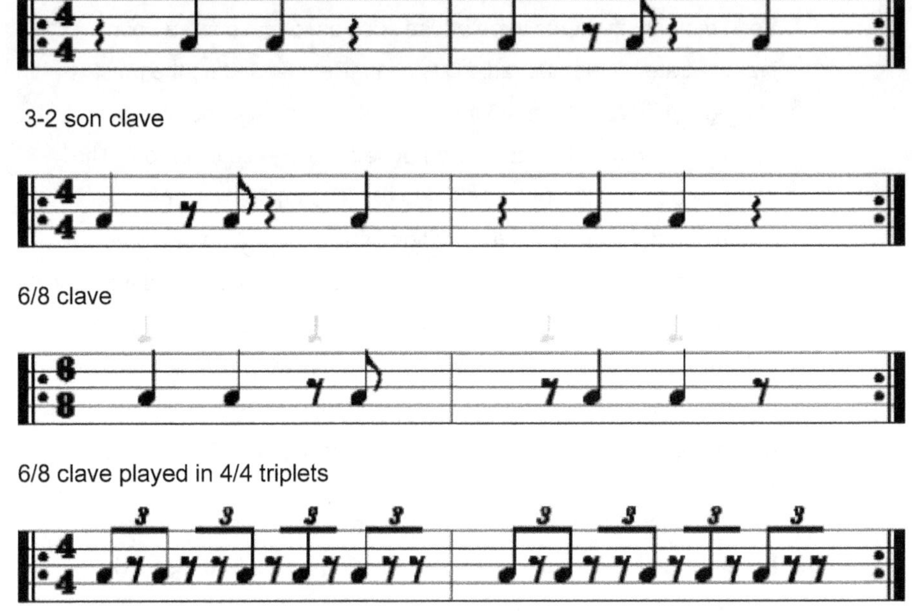

3-2 son clave

6/8 clave

6/8 clave played in 4/4 triplets

The normal composition of a salsa song and rhythm is based around core instruments of trumpet, bongo, conga, double bass, piano, campana or timbales, guiro, cowbell and clave. More modern salsa orchestras use saxophone. In danzones and son music, violins were played at certain times.

The music hasn't changed much since the 19th century style of salsa music apart from the rhythm, which has speeded up and a few more instruments have been included. Originally, son, which came before salsa, used just bongos, a tres guitar, maracas and claves. Arsenio Rodriques added The Rough Guide To Cuban Music congas to the orchestra and gave it a more rounded feel. When salsa went to New York, more instruments were added such as to make salsa sound jazzier. Later in the 60s radio DJs and MCs speeded up the music by playing the 78 records at 45 speed, although this was nothing new because the original danzon is supposed to increase in tempo. The music of danzon is very important to understand the base of salsa because a danzon has all the sections that establish salsa music. Danzón is both elegant and virtuosic music (and dance). A danzón, in its original form, does not feature any improvisations, unlike most other popular Cuban genres. A danzón has the following typical structure (which stems from European rondo): Rondeau (music) -- Medieval and Renaissance form. (Wikipedia) Danzón Overview).

Cuba's national dance (danzón) is the product of centuries of evolution and transformation, from its roots in the French contredanse to its spawning of the mambo and the cha-cha-chá. Considered part of Cuba's classical music lineage—and one of the primary ancestors of popular music on the island, the danzón represents a bygone era yet remains connected to its musical family throughout the Americas.

In 17th-century France and England, court dances were common practice among the social elite. The French *contredanse* and the English country-dance both became primordial influences in Cuban culture as Europeans went west to the Caribbean. In Cuba, the contredanse became the *contradanza criolla* (Creole contredanse), and by the late 18th century the style was adopted and the word "criolla" was dropped. The first instrumental group to play contradanzas was the *orquesta típica*, consisting of woodwinds, brass, strings, the tympani and the Cuban gourd scraper known as the *güiro*. A signature element in the music is a five-note rhythmical pattern called the *cinquillo (National Geographic online)*.

A Breakdown of Danzon Musical Rhythm:

- An introduction or paseo (A), usually 16 measures.
- The theme or principal melody (B), featuring the flute, thus often referred to as parte de (la) flauta ("flute part").
- A repeat of the introduction.
- The trio (C), featuring the strings, thus also called parte del violín ("violin part").
- This could either be a clichéd ending (there are a few standard danzón endings), another repeat of the introduction, or a combination of both.

The classic form is thus ABAC or ABACA. A danzón-chá or danzón-mambo typically adds another part (D), an open vamp in which soloists can improvise, creating an ABACD or, more commonly, ABACAD.

REVIEW:
1. Who added percussion of congas to the danzon?
2. From where did the contredanse originate?
3. What influence did English Country dancing have on salsa?

Chapter 3

In this chapter you learn about:

- different teaching styles
- your type of personality
- which teaching style suits your personality
- effective means of communication
- learning styles

Your Guide to Becoming a Qualified Salsa Teacher

"No one can be myself like I can, for this job Im the best man"
Chesney Hawkes, No 1 in the UK pop charts March 1991

The Different Teaching Styles
There are teaching 3 styles you can use to teach salsa dance: Each style has advantages and disadvantages.

Your Personality

It is important to be true to your own personality when teaching. This will enthuse your students with your own passion for the dance. If you are not true to your own personality, the students will notice that there is a lack of authenticity in what you are doing and saying and they may not entrust in you their confidence because of this. The teacher must also consider the setting in which they want to teach salsa and also the audience. If you are teaching in a secondary school and your audience are young people aged under 16, your teaching style may have to be different to that of a group who are all over the age of 18 at a night club. The expectations, behaviour and most importantly, the law relating to the students will be different and may require a different teaching style.

Which style of salsa do you want to teach?

Your Guide to Becoming a Qualified Salsa Teacher

1 Cuban style focuses on basic steps with good body movement and interpretation of the music. It has been said that Cuban style is more about freedom and having fun. The author believes that all styles of social dance should be fun and it is down to the teacher to make it interesting and fun for the students regardless of the style of dance.

2 LA style is about the dancers' attitude, and flashy spins and dips.

3 New York style is about being always on the beat and the follower strictly following the leader. Technique and timing are paramount in this style.

4 Colombian style is very fast and acrobatic. It requires a high degree of fitness and coordination. The Colombian style is based around swing, jazz and Cuban Colombia footwork also called Pachanga and Boogaloo.

There are others styles of salsa but the Cuban, LA and New York styles are most prevalent with the Colombian style as a well known but less commercial style of salsa.

Different Teaching Styles You Can Use To Engage Your Students.

Authoritarian: this is also known as autocratic and dictatorial. The teacher tells the student what, when, how, with who and where to do the steps and moves. The student doesn't have much choice in the execution of what they are doing. They can only decide to follow or not to follow the instructions from the teacher.

Advantages: The students have less chance of getting it wrong if they are following exactly what the teacher is instructing. There is not much room for making mistakes. This teaching style demands the attention and respect of the student.

Disadvantages: The students don't have a chance to absorb the information in their own way and in their own time. Students might need less structure and more thinking time. The teacher may be too demanding and possibly lose the students' respect.

Laissez faire: The teacher allows the students a lot of freedom to experiment with different ways of learning and the students are given different ways of learning the steps and moves. The teacher is relaxed and is not too concerned if the student doesn't understand straight away.

Advantages: The students have a chance to absorb the information in their own way and in their own time. There is flexibility of learning.

Disadvantages: The students don't always respect a teacher who lets them do more or less what they want to do. The students may be confused because of the lack of direction.

Democratic: The teachers asks everyone what they would like to learn and gives them choice. In this teaching style the teacher frequently asks the students opinion on what they want to learn.

Advantages: The students feel part of the learning process and feel empowered. The student can choose what best suits their learning style.

Your Guide to Becoming a Qualified Salsa Teacher

Disadvantages: The students may not want to make any decisions and might prefer full instructions from the teacher or other students. Students may just not vote for what they want and opt out.

Effective communication

Teaching styles vary but you will need good communication skills to be an effective teacher. The following qualities are important for teaching:

Openness

Integrity

Authenticity/vulnerability

Politeness

Thinking fast and sometimes speaking fast

Tell interesting stories

Clarify points with energy

Don't pause with ums and ahs

Dress appropriately

Be fluid in your speaking

Be creative

Speak with conviction

Be competent

Use good visuals

Be a risk taker when necessary

Good eye contact

An authoritative voice

Learning Styles

The different learning styles of students:

You must take into account the learning styles of the students in class, everyone is different:

Here are 4 different learning styles:

Visual:
learn best by watching and following directly without much explanation or instruction.

Audio:
need to be told exactly what to do and need to have the music on as they do it to learn properly.

Read/write:
like the moves written down so they can think about them and remember them.

Kinaesthetic:
have to do the moves and feel the sensation of the move before it becomes second nature. People with a strong kinaesthetic ability are normally best suited to dance because body movement is almost entirely about the physical feeling.

Your Guide to Becoming a Qualified Salsa Teacher

REVIEW:

1. Name 5 qualities of communication which are effective for teaching?
2. Why is it important to stay true to your personality when teaching?
3. What are the fundamental steps in the LA/NY American style salsa?

There are three basic teaching styles. Authoritarian, Laissez faire and Democratic. Which one(s) suit your personality?

There are four different learning styles. Visual, Audio, Read/write and Kinaesthetic: Which one do you rely on most when learning?

There are 4 main styles of salsa: Cuban, Colombian, LA and New York. Which is your preferred style of salsa and which teaching style would be compatible with it?

It's important to note that every situation in teaching requires a slightly different approach. Flexibility and variety of teaching style is required in most situations.

Chapter 4

In this chapter you learn about:

- the advantages of being a qualified salsa teacher
- examinations you can take and coverage of the syllabus
- anatomy and why its important to know it
- the choice of fulltime and part time teaching

Your Guide to Becoming a Qualified Salsa Teacher

"Be everywhere, do everything, and never fail to astonish the customer"

169 Margaret Getchell, Macys Mots.

STARTING YOUR TEACHING PRACTICE

The Rules and Regulations, Teaching Practice Liability Insurance and
Health and Safety

The rules and regulations for teaching dance are tightening every year.
The law regarding teaching any person in a public place requires the
following:
Teaching practice liability insurance, to obtain this you require a
qualification and or membership to a professional training body. To
obtain a qualification and membership of a professional body you require
training and knowledge of your subject and practical and theoretical
class management skills. Some of these skills can only be obtained by
experience.

Depending on where you teach you may require music licences, PPL –
Phonographic Performance Limited and PRS – Performing Rights
Society.

Your Guide to Becoming a Qualified Salsa Teacher

If you teach for the school or education system you will require *Child protection training. The NSPCC "aims to support individual and organisational learning and aim to keep children safe. They do this by providing a range of services for health, social services, local councils, education, voluntary groups and Child protection police checks".* You should draw up a child protection policy. You should refer to the Children Act 2004 and its guidelines. It is an obligation on all teachers to keep records of all students including the date of birth, address and any medical conditions. This register must also be used in emergency evacuation procedures. If working with a school as part of the school curriculum, you should inform the Head Teacher of the school of any suspected form of abuse that a child may portray.

First Aid certificates can be obtained at very low cost from the British Red Cross and St John Ambulance Service.
http://www.sja.org.uk/sja/training-courses.aspx

CRB disclosure applications can be obtained from www.crb.gov.uk they state that *"the current legislation does not allow the self-employed or individuals to apply for a CRB check on themselves".* If you have been asked to apply for a CRB check you will need to speak to the person who asked you to apply as they will be able to provide you with the application form.
Standard Disclosure. This is primarily available to anyone working with children or vulnerable adults. Standard Disclosures show current and spent convictions, cautions, reprimands and warnings held on the Police National Computer. If the post involves working with children or vulnerable adults, the following may also be searched: Protection of

Children Act (POCA) List, Protection of Vulnerable Adults (POVA) List. Umbrella organisations are enlisted to administer the CRB check. A list of these organisations can be found on the www.crb.gov.uk website. The cost of the CRB check is between £31 and £36 exclusive of the umbrella organisations administration fee which could be between £10 and £20.

REVIEW:
1. Where can you obtain public liability insurance?
2. To play music publicly, what do you require?
3. Where can you obtain a) first aid training b) CRB checks and verification?

Teaching for the private sector

Teaching for the private sector is where you can teach for night clubs with an adult population or for wine bars and social clubs where the average age is over 18. Most social clubs and night clubs for adults have their own PPL and PRS Licences. UK copyright law (primarily, the Copyright, Designs and Patents Act 1988) provides protection for recorded music and music videos (along with other types of creative works,) by giving the copyright owner certain exclusive rights of use. Anyone who uses recorded music or music videos for those protected uses will be infringing copyright unless they are licensed (i.e. authorised) to do so by the copyright owner. PPLUK.COM PPL is not the same as the Performing Right Society (PRS), the Mechanical Copyright Protection Society (MCPS) or the MCPS-PRS Alliance.

Whenever a sound recording or music video is played in public or broadcast in the UK, a PRS license is likely to be required in addition to a license from PPL. Similarly, you are likely to need a PPL license as well as an MCPS license to copy a sound recording or music video in the UK. Check out www.ppluk.com to apply for your music rights in the UK.

Regarding music licences, it is the teachers' obligation to check this because they are personally responsible for their actions if they hire a night club hall.

To begin with, when starting to teach in a nightclub or wine bar environment, legally you must consider who your student audience will be. Are they over the age of 16? If they are not, are they accompanied by a guardian? Who is the bar supervisor or manager and have they explained the health and safety procedure to you? Do you need door staff security for your classes? If your classes include a nightclub element of dancing for the teaching practice then you or the club owner must pay for door staff? For every fifty people who attend your teaching practice event there must be one door staff. This figure of fifty varies depending on the city or town council in which you intend to teach. The only exception to this is where you have a membership scheme which will makes the event a private and not a public event. Alternatively if the event involves classes throughout the night and the teacher is supervising the whole night then this can be considered teaching as opposed to a night club party. It is important to check with your local council to confirm specific regulations and local town policies.

Risk Assessment:

Hazards and safety checks. As the hirer of a private club or bar, you as the hirer must make your own hazard and safety checks. It is the teachers' legal responsibility to look for potential hazards in the teaching environment. Typical examples of hazards are as follows:

Floor surfaces: are they even? Is it carpet, tiled wooden floor, is the floor sprung? Is the floor too slippery or resistant to movement?

Access and exits: are pathways safe free from obstruction? Where are the fire extinguishers?

Where are the fire exits? Are these obscured?

Stairs: are they safe for the teaching practice? Is there disabled access?

Lighting: is it bright enough for people to see clearly?

Your Guide to Becoming a Qualified Salsa Teacher

Air quality: is there air conditioning or adequate ventilation?
Condition of sanitary and hygiene facilities: Do the toilets work and are
they clean?
Use of equipment: Are all the plug sockets safe? When were they last
tested?
Is there clean drinking water? The public have a right to clean drinking
water regardless of whether it is a private or teaching practice
organisation under the Licensing Act 2003.
In essence is the building being used safe? The risk assessment plan
should state all the areas to be used and equipment as well as any other
areas. The assessment should be dated, the time stated and signed by
the person who checked the risk.

Teaching for the public sector:
Teaching for the public sector requires you to be twice as thorough as
the private sector regarding rules and regulations. In addition to the law,
teaching practice bodies have very stringent policies in relation to the
teaching practice and have a high duty of care and expectation of
standards of quality.

The need for certification, the benefits of being qualified and insured

Anyone that wants to teach dance in the public sector must have a level
of certification to say that the person teaching is a valid teacher. The
person must be certified by a professional body to maintain a standard of
expertise and professionalism. Once the person is qualified that person

may then acquire teaching practice liability insurance for any injury or damages incurred by teaching practice as a result of the teacher. Insurance companies are reluctant to insure dance teachers if they are not qualified because if you are not qualified you are seen as a high risk because you have not proved that you can teach safely or with established knowledge of the subject.

National teaching bodies are: the RSA, The Council for Dance Education and Training (the national standards body of the professional dance industry), the (ISTD) Imperial Society of Teachers of Dancing, (IDTA) International Dance Teachers Association, (UKA) United Kingdom Alliance of Professional Teachers of Dancing and Kindred Arts. For teaching in maintained schools you would require the QTS: Qualified Teacher Status.

The topics covered in the Theory part of the UKA course include:

The levels of salsa teaching: student, associate, licentiate and fellowship.

Qualities of a good teacher:
Of the many qualities a good teacher requires patience is the most important. Good communication skills are essential for the success of a teacher.

Preparation for a class: A lesson plan is important if you want to be a good teacher. A plan should be SMART: specific, measurable, achievable, results based and time specific. The plan should breakdown what you want to teach, how long each section should take to complete and what resources you want to use. It should also include your aim and outcome/objectives for your class. I.e. the students should be able to do the basic mambo and side step in time with the music.

Psychology: Are the students psychologically prepared for the lesson? How do they learn? This will be covered in the following chapters.

How to criticise:

The students' ability to learn will be based largely on their ability to give feedback when they don't understand something. If the students believe that they are not able to freely say they don't understand or are too nervous to ask questions, then this will limit their potential for learning. The teacher must make the students feel comfortable enough to ask questions and give feedback. The teacher shouldn't make fun of the students or laugh at them. This would be extremely unprofessional. It is better to say to the students what they are doing right and state what can be improved instead of emphasising the fault. Constructive criticism is the best option.

"Any fool can criticize, condemn and complain but it takes character and self control to be understanding and forgiving." Dale Carnegie.

Class management:

If there is a class of 30 students in a small room you have the options of putting people in lines, in a horseshoe shape or in a big circle. The shape of the class depends also on the moves you want to teach and making sure that everyone can see and hear properly.

Teaching as your business

Your Guide to Becoming a Qualified Salsa Teacher

This will be covered in later chapters which will include the marketing, advertising, finance and legalities of the business side of teaching.

History of Salsa music and Dance:
Explained in the earlier chapters it is important to know the history of salsa so that students have some context for what they are learning.

Music Analysis and Rhythmic knowledge
Previous chapters covered the development and structure of salsa music and rhythm. You must demonstrate knowledge of bars, phrases and notes. Reference should also be given to the clave rhythm. Basic music notation is useful to understanding the rhythms of salsa and especially the clave. Salsa music is played over 8 beats, called a phrase. These phrases are split into 2 bars or measures of 4 beats each. On a musical notation sheet you will see notes on a staff, which are played by musical instruments. In salsa you will hear a 4/4 time signature but in some of the clave rhythms you will hear some variation of 6/8.

The differences between the Salsa Styles:
As you will now know, there are many styles of salsa dance but they all originated in Cuba before developing and changing.

Comparison of the different Latin Rhythms
For teachers who are non musicians this will be one of the more difficult parts of the course. You should be able to differentiate between mambo, cha cha cha, merengue and other Latin dance rhythms.

Child Protection

Your Guide to Becoming a Qualified Salsa Teacher

There should be an awareness of child protection procedures. Training
and information on this subject can be obtained from the NSPCC.

Professional Code of conduct:
Depending on which organisation you join there will be different codes of
conduct. The UKA require that you follow their guidelines diligently. It is
mainly concerned with child protection, health and safety and ensuring
that the law is followed in respect of public liability.

The topics covered in the Practical part of the course include:

Introduction to a class
How to break down the basic steps
How to explain the Salsa rhythm to complete beginners
How to explain the holds
How to explain a turn versus spin
How to construct a basic Salsa dance in both Cuban and Cross-body
Style

All the participants will be asked to teach a routine in front of a group of
people.

In addition to the above dance teaching qualifications a good teacher will
also aim for higher recognised academic teaching qualifications. This is
usually called a Certificate in Education, or Postgraduate Certificate in
Education PGCE. You can do a degree in dance and continue with a
Masters degree. These qualifications would require a more in depth

knowledge of physiology and teaching theory. To work in maintained schools everyone requires a QTS: Qualified Teaching Status.

For teaching adults only, it is sufficient to obtain a diploma from the UKA: United Kingdom Alliance. The UKA course cost is £210 plus the invigilators travel expenses to the testing centre. (2008).

Anatomy: On the next page we will look at the major bones and muscles of the body. Test your knowledge by linking the names to the body parts.

Major muscles of
the body:

Sterno mastoid
Trapezius
Deltoid
Pectoralis major
Triceps/ biceps

latimus dorsi
External and
internal obliques
Rectus abdominus
Sarcospinalis
Gluteus maximus
Adductor magnus
Llliopsoas
Sartorius
Rectus femoris
Hamstrings
Gastocnemius
Tebialis anterior
Soleus

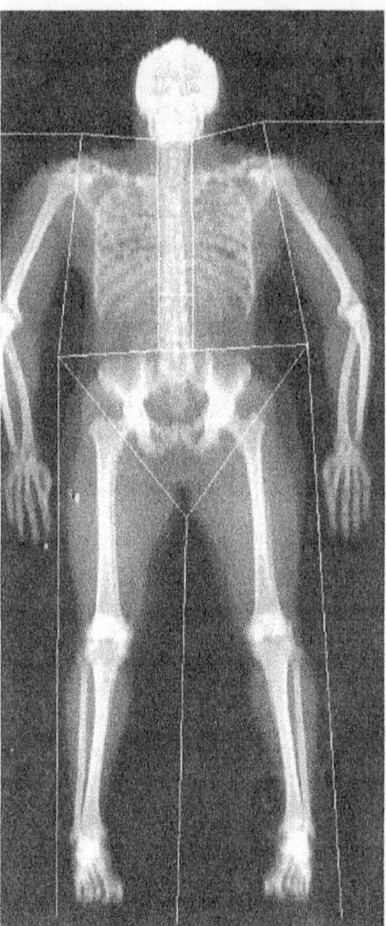

Birmingham Sports Science Dept 2009.
Thomas O'flaherty.

The parallel bones
in the body:
Skull
Cervical vertebrae
Clavicle
Scapula
Thorax
Humerus
Sternum
Vertebra
Sacrum
Coccy
Pelvic girdle
Ulna
Radius
Carpals/
Metacarpals
Femur
Patella
Tibia
Fibula
Talus
Tarsals/
Metatarsals

Anatomy

Functions of the skeleton: 1. Support and strength, 2. attachment for muscle. 3. levers. 4. protection for soft body parts.

Movement of the body is brought about by action of the muscles on the bones, which act as levers.
The actions of the muscles consist of:

1 Flexion: bending or decreasing the angle,

2 Extension: bending stretching/straightening

3 Hyperextension: extension carried beyond the normal range of motion/anatomical position.

4 Abduction: moving the body part away from the centre line, e.g. raising the arm.

5 Adduction: bringing the body part back to the centre line, lowering the arm to the side.

6 Supination: raising and turning the body part, rotating upwards and outwards.

7 Pronation: lowering and turning, rotating the body part, downwards and inwards.

8 Rotation: pivoting the body part inwards or outwards around a long axis, rolling the head.

9 Circumduction: a complete circular motion of the body, circling the arm at the shoulder.

10 Eversion: turning the body part outwards, foot.

11 Inversion: turning the body part inwards.

Under flexion you also have: dorsiflexion: turning the toes up towards the shins and plantarflexion: pointing the toes.

A joint and its structures may be harmed when:
1) movements go beyond the desired range of motion; 2) movements are performed incorrectly 3) movements are performed too fast without proper body control.

Joints: prolonged training can cause thickening of the cartilage. Severe or uneven stress can wear the cartilage away and restrict the movement of the joint. (A reference manual for teachers of dance exercise J May 1988)

Warm ups: why do them?
The teacher should be well acquainted with the most common injury sites in salsa dance. The shoulder, the wrist, the ankle, shin, knee and lower back are prone to injury in partner dancing and salsa is no exception. "After warming up in exercise, there is a temporary thickening of the articular cartilage and the synovial fluid membrane stimulates the release of the synovial fluid lubricating the joints." p11 (J May 1988). This action dramatically reduces the chances of injury. Warm ups are required to protect the body from the stresses and strains of salsa dancing.

The teacher should ensure the students are wearing appropriate footwear. An open shoe, with no support around the ankle,   is dangerous in salsa dancing. The turning and twisting could cause a twisted ankle.

Your Guide to Becoming a Qualified Salsa Teacher

A warm down or cool down is also needed to restore normality to the heart rate and prevent venous pooling of blood in the lower limbs. P56 (J May 1988). You should have knowledge of all the major bones and muscles of the body and know their function. You should also know the main points of injury when dancing salsa. You should be able to explain the need for warm ups and cool downs.

Here is a list of the main bones and muscles in the human body: consider these when you are preparing for a dance teaching examination Skull, clavicle, cervical vertebrae, scapula, thorax, sternum, humerus, ulna, radius, metacarpals, sternum, vertebrae, sacrum, coccy, pelvic girdle, femur, patella, fibula, tibia, talus, tarsals and metatarsals.

The various major muscles of the human body: trapezius, deltoids, latimuss dorsi, bicep, tricep, brachialis cover the upper body. The gluteus maximus, abdominals, obliques, erectors spinea, flexors and abductors cover the mid section and hips. The gastrocnemius, solarius and plantaris cover the lower leg muscles known as the calf.

You should know the function of these muscles, considering whether they are more prone to injury in partner dance.

Review:

1. What are the four functions of the skeleton?
2. What are the eleven actions of the muscles?
3. Why should you warm up before exercise?
4. Why should you warm down after exercise?

Your Guide to Becoming a Qualified Salsa Teacher

To teach is to learn twice" Joseph Joubert, Pensees

What type of teacher do you want to be?

Earlier we looked at the different leadership teacher styles. We also looked at how teaching should be part of your personality makeup and should be an extension of who you are as a person. If you are a happy go lucky person who likes to tell jokes and is very relaxed in their approach to teaching, it wouldn't make sense to adapt a teaching style which was authoritarian and forced students to follow the instructions blindly. It is possible to teach a very technical move with an element of fun and entertainment. What this would mean in practice is that the moves would have to be broken down into small chunks and only small amounts of information can be passed onto the students each time. The alternative is to be very strict and dictate 100% focus on the task of learning lots of moves or detailed technique without much student interaction or engagement. This teaching style is authoritarian and can put some people off learning although people who are really serious about learning thoroughly and efficiently might prefer this style of teaching. This is why the first thing you do when teaching a salsa dance class or any subject for that matter is to make an initial assessment of the students' ability.

Your goals, short and long term, aims and objectives.

The fact that you're reading this book means that you are either already teaching salsa dance or are ready to start to learn to teach salsa dance. You must define your aims as a teacher from your short term goals to long term goals. Use the next page to write down your teaching goals.

Your Teaching Goals.

Short term   Long term

1

2

3

4

5

6

7

8

9

10

Your Guide to Becoming a Qualified Salsa Teacher

How often do you want to teach?

Only teach in the evening and be a part time teacher?
If this is the case then your focus would be suitable within a gymnasium
studio or night club/restaurant bar. The advantages and disadvantages
of these venues will be explained in the case studies in the following
pages.

Teach full time in the day and evening?
Being a fulltime teacher will require much more preparation and session
planning. You have much more choice regarding work opportunities.
You can put yourself up for hire at teaching practice and private
organisations and teach for one hour or a couple of hours in the
afternoon. You decide how much you charge the group and it is
reasonable to charge between £80 and £120 for between one and two
hours. The Arts Council of England suggests a daily artist rate of £175.
Only you can decide your value based on your unique experience, level
of qualifications and teaching style.

Start your own dance school and eventually hire other teachers?
A natural progression would be to start your own dance school in a fixed
location. This would allow you to build your reputation and client base.
There are many teachers in the world but very few own or run a dance
school. The reason being is that the running of the dance school would
involve you in lots of administration and financial commitment the stress
of which may put you off teaching dance all together.
To start off you could hire a studio space for periods of a month at a
time. Then if there is a good up take of students and interest in your

classes, you can rent the space for six months and test the water on development of the classes. Once you have six months rental behind you this should give you a good indication of whether you should take on a yearly tenancy or even longer. If a dance school is your long term goal, then student development should be your ultimate aim because your students will develop their own dance skills in time and may want to teach or even perform themselves. Some of your students may even set up their own dance school before you do. Some of the subjects regarding setting up your own dance school will be covered in the following case studies.

Do you want to choreograph dance pieces for shows and performances? Choreographing is one of the most challenging but also satisfying things you can do in dance. If you choreograph for yourself or other people it is a creative process which demonstrates your creativity, artistic interpretation and cements your values as a dance teacher. Teaching choreography will also test your leadership skills, your empathy and patience with people. To perform in front of your peers is a real test of character whether you are a dancer or choreographer. You are opening yourself up for criticism. Your competitors will try and disrupt, steal your ideas and destroy your dancers' confidence. But you may even gain your competitors' respect if your choreography is good and they might hire you to perform for them. Confidence is the one thing that will make or break a performance. A dancers' confidence must be rooted in their own ability. "Believe in yourself, have faith in your abilities. Without a humble but reasonable confidence in your own powers, you cannot be successful or happy." (Norman Vincent Peale, philosophers notes).

Your Guide to Becoming a Qualified Salsa Teacher

We all have hang-ups and insecurities and lack confidence either in our looks or dance ability. Sometimes these insecurities are used to blame other dancers or the choreographer that can destroy team building. There is nothing worse than dancers who don't trust or believe in their choreographer because these dancers will undermine the whole performance and never give 100% commitment. The choreographer must get to know the dancers personally. Find out their lifestyle, their likes and dislikes and their aims and needs in dance. It may be the case that a student is incredibly shy when it comes to dancing in public but has always dreamed of performing in front of a crowd. The journey for them would be an incredibly hard but fulfilling one and you should never underestimate your value as a teacher to them. You can make peoples' dreams come true if you really value yourself as a teacher and value your students as people.

Only teach adults?

There are advantages and disadvantages to teaching adults. The advantages are that they have disposable income to afford the class themselves. Salsa is a social dance which means some people do it with the aim of finding a partner. They may keep coming to the class until they find that partner. Adults like the routine of a social activity to look forward to and break up what may be quite a boring week. The disadvantages are that because they are adults they have many distractions in their lives and they may not give you 100% attention or commitment to learning. If your classes are held in a club, the students may have had one drink too many and their balance, coordination and timing, all the things which are required in dance would be lost. To further this point, if a person is tipsy in a class this may cause disruptions you will be lucky if you get 50% of their attention. If the student is not paying attention, then they are wasting their money and you as a teacher are wasting your time. If you are teaching in a bar, nightclub or restaurant environment, there is a strong likelihood that people have been drinking and some may be tipsy or even drunk. If there is an accident because of the drunk person not following instructions and the drunk person tries for example to dip another person and that person slips a disc or falls and fractures a bone, the teacher is responsible because they ignored the risk assessment of letting a drunk person lead another person into a dangerous movement.

Salsa is a partner dance where there is one leader and one follower. If either the leader or follower is not paying attention and goes off on a frolic of their own, you, as the teacher, are indirectly authorising whatever happens to your students. Students in the class trust you as a qualified dance teacher and expect you to instruct them safely. The follower dances with the leader on the basis that the instructor is supervising the class. The follower should not delegate that trust to a leader who is drunk and doesn't know what they are doing. If you are not observing the students enough, people can get injured and they will not hesitate to make a personal injury claim against you. In the event you are teaching a hen party where it is expected that your participants are going to get drunk or very tipsy before the workshop, you have to balance the risk or the movements that you want to teach and the level of coordination and control the members of the hen party may have.

 Only teach children?

The law: Any teacher, even a newly-qualified one, should be expected to have Qualified Teacher Status (QTS). To work lawfully as a qualified teacher in a maintained school or non-maintained special school, teachers need to have QTS, apart from certain exceptions. QTS is a status, granted to teachers who have demonstrated that they have met the required professional standards to be able to teach in maintained schools, non-maintained special schools or pupil referral units in England.

Overseas Trained Teachers (OTTs):
 Overseas trained teachers are allowed to work as unqualified teachers for a maximum of four years without the need to gain QTS. This four year period begins on the first day that a teacher takes up their post in a maintained school or non-maintained special school and expires four calendar years later. If an overseas trained teacher (OTT) wishes to be awarded QTS, they will need to have had the award made before their four year exemption period ends.

Instructors
Instructors are "unqualified teachers" who the law allows to carry out the same duties as qualified teachers. (Reference www.cdet.org.uk).

The advantages to teaching children
Children can be very attentive and absorb information very quickly. Some children may even take up dance as one of their main subjects in secondary school and become teachers themselves in the future. The pupils often have opportunities to present what they know in the form of an end of term performance or show. This can focus their minds and also give them an immense boost of self esteem.

Your Guide to Becoming a Qualified Salsa Teacher

The disadvantages to teaching children

The disadvantages are that if you are teaching dance in an elementary or secondary school some of the pupils may not have chosen to do the activity or may have chosen it by default because they wanted to get out of other subjects. If this is the case pupils may well play up and totally disrupt your class. Your objective then has to be to get the pupils attention and instruct them with sufficient authority to get them to follow what you say. To teach in schools you require CRB checks and disclosures and training in child protection. You should have a child protection policy that can be given to all parents to read before their children join the course.

The QTS Qualification will cover all of these areas: Relationships with children and young people, communicating and working with others, Personal professional development, Teaching and learning, Assessment and monitoring, Subjects and curriculum, Literacy, numeracy and ICT, Achievement and diversity, Planning, Teaching, Assessing, monitoring and giving feedback, Reviewing, teaching and learning, Learning environment and Team working and collaboration.

Teach all age groups?

It is possible in some teaching practice community events for you to teach adults, young people and children. Provided there is supervision from the parents and guardians of the children, there is less provision for child protection and CRB verification however it is always good practice to have a qualification and insurance to cover you for any teaching practice liability. It is not good practice to teach children salsa in a nightclub, or restaurant environment without the children's parent or guardian. You are teaching the general public and you can't vet who comes to your classes off the street. In adult environments, children should always be accompanied by their parent or guardian. The teacher should not leave themselves open to negligence acts of their students. Be firm with parents and students who would like to join the class and explain the health and safety and child protection procedures to them.

Maslow's Hierarchy of Needs

According to Abraham Maslow in his 1943 paper *A Theory of Human Motivation*, there are five levels of needs of the learner. "Physiological needs are fundamental, while the top levels are termed growth needs associated with psychological needs. Deficiency needs must be met first. Once these are met, seeking to satisfy growth needs drives personal growth." (http://en.wikipedia.org/wiki/Maslow's_hierarchy_of_needs.). Level 1) survival; 2) security; 3) belonging; 4) self-esteem; and 5) self-fulfilment.

If equal opportunity legislation and policy isn't followed the Maslow's hierarchy even at level 1 cannot be satisfied because the learner would feel threatened for their survival if there are threats to the race, sex, sexual orientation, faith, religion or disability. Under current legislation the learner has rights. These rights include the right to be treated equally under the Race Relations Act 1976, The Sex Discrimination Act 1975 and the Human Rights Act, The Disability Discrimination Act 1995 and Data Protection Act 1998. These are only some of the acts which apply to the learner rights which protect them in adult education. The tutor must be an equal opportunities endorser. They must create a safe environment for everybody.

Creating Ground Rules for the Students and Yourself as the Teacher

Ground rules are made to establish a base point for both teacher and learner. It is an informal contract for learning and teaching. The ground rules establish what is not tolerated and what should be provided. For example, the language used in the class must not be offensive. In effect any ground rules must adhere to the equal opportunities policies of the city council and law regarding education. There must also be agreement of how the students want to be treated. Rules such as no drinking of alcohol, smoking or illegal drug use. The students must not turn up drunk or stoned and likewise the tutor! With reference to teaching dance, it would be a ground rule that everyone does a warm-up up for their own safety, because if the learner becomes injured, this puts the tutor at risk of a personal injury claim. If the tutor talks to a student in a disrespectful manner, the student should also have a right to refer to the ground rules and ask the tutor to stick to them. The ground rules apply to both the teacher and the student. Ground rules need to be agreed at the very beginning and any breach must be dealt with immediately because if they are not, the student or teacher will assume that it is ok to continue breaching them.

Your Guide to Becoming a Qualified Salsa Teacher

Ground Rules Agreement:

1 Not drink alcohol excessively before or during the dance class

2 Not smoke inside the building premises.

3 Not use illegal drugs on the premises

4 Not molest or handle inappropriately other students or staff.

5 Treat everyone equally regardless of sex, race, religion, faith, colour, sexual orientation or disability.

6 Ensure children should always be accompanied by their parent or guardian.

7 Report any dangerous hazards or accidents immediately to a teacher or staff member for everybody's safety.

8 Inform the teacher of any injuries or health problems which affect your dance ability.

9 Be polite and respect everyone in the class.

10 Not publicise alternative dance classes or events on the premises without the principle teachers' agreement.

Signed: ....Dated: ......Name in Capitals: ....

Your Guide to Becoming a Qualified Salsa Teacher

The Role of a Dance Teacher

The role of the dance teacher, is to transfer skills and to share knowledge with the students. In order to be effective in this role, the teacher must have good communication skills, and be able to create a rapport with the students.

  Dance is a form of communication and expression therefore the tutors' aim is to provide the technique in dance, so eventually the student can think for themselves and create their own dance movements. The students needs must be ascertained, their aims and outcomes specified and an assessment of their level of ability.

Student A intends to go on holiday to Cuba and wants to prepare by learning salsa to enhance their social skills.

Their aim is to improve their social skills with the outcome of learning to salsa dance. Student B has always dreamed of being a dancer and wants to perform in salsa shows and demonstrations. Student B's aims and outcomes will be staged differently and assessed differently. Student A will be taught more about the etiquette of salsa partner dancing whereas student B will be taught the importance of strong performance technique. Student Bs' path is longer a lot harder. Student B will require much encouragement, more independent learning, constant evaluation, and one to one support. Student A would need to know the basics of social dancing and how to dance socially with a wide range of people.

Your Guide to Becoming a Qualified Salsa Teacher

The teacher tutor must be approachable and presentable. Presentation is how most people, including students, judge you regardless of knowledge or ability. To teach dance a teacher must be qualified in their specific area with a nationally recognised body and have teaching practice liability insurance. In addition, the tutor must adhere to the law. The teacher must keep records of the students' attendance, their goals and aims. The teacher must set out ground rules so that the students and tutor know their boundaries. The tutor should not use their position of power to exploit the student and both the student and tutor should not breach health and safety, equal opportunity rules regarding race, sex, sexual orientation, faith, religion or disability. For example, if a student said something homophobic to another student, in the first instance of a ground rule break the tutor must remind the student to the ground rules. If repeated breaches occur the tutor must refer to their line manager to address the issue.

If a fight breaks out in the dance class.
The tutor must evacuate the room where the incident is occurring and not become physically involved. The Health and safety at Work Act 1974 must be adhered to. The line manager and house security must be alerted immediately.

Encourage learners to stay on a course to achieve their aims.

The first step in encouraging the learner to stay on course is to find out where the student is in their class and ask them for feedback. This will help the teacher assess the situation and be better able to target the student's aims and outcomes. The teacher's feedback to the student must always be constructive.

If a student aims to be able to perform a dance in front of their friends and family at a social occasion, the teacher must assess if the student has confidence in their abilities to fulfil these outcomes; to dance in time with the music, have a variety of steps, have good posture and be relaxed dancing in public. The teacher should tell the student what they are doing right and also what they can improve upon.

The teacher can encourage the student further by reminding them of what they have learnt so far and congratulate them on achieving these outcomes. The teacher can encourage the student to keep individual learning logs of what they have learnt. The teacher can write out learning plan for the student to fill in after the class. The teacher can give the student 1-1 support and attention. The teacher can improve the students' self esteem by acknowledging their past achievements.

An awareness of the learning cycle,
From the moment a student walks through your door and asks to join your dance school or class, you as a teacher must establish their level with an initial assessment which can be done straight way. You should ask your students about any injury or impairments that may affect their learning. Ask them about any previous dance experience and what their aims and objectives are.

REVIEW:

1 What is the purpose of having ground rules?

2 How do you encourage students to stay on course and keep attending?

3 In what year was the health and safety act passed?

Your Guide to Becoming a Qualified Salsa Teacher

Motivations for Learning Salsa:

weight loss,
social activity,
meet the opposite sex,
learn about the culture of salsa,
become a salsa dance performer,
become a teacher!
curiousity, to try something new.

Whatever the students' motivations, the teacher should be aware of
these to prepare properly and establish if their aims are realistic and
achievable. It might be the case that the type of class you plan to teach
and the way you intend to teach would not be appropriate for the student.
This is the point of an initial assessment, to find out how you can help the
student.

Once the student has started doing the classes, there will come a point
when they will need to develop onto a higher level; from beginner to level
2 beginners or intermediate level. It is not encouraging for the student to
attend classes where they are supposed to be learning and they stay at
the same level for months or even years. If the students' aim is just to
have fun and meet people and they are using the class only for
socialising then the teacher has to look at their own aims and purposes
for teaching salsa. Salsa cannot be learnt efficiently by just doing it once
a week with no practice in between. Like most things, the mind and body

need practice until the action or thought becomes a reflex action. Only then can a student know they are competent at how to dance salsa.

Obtain feedback

When the student is doing the steps, moves or following an instruction, it is imperative that the teacher is observing closely because if they are not then the student learns incorrectly and it is very hard to undo people's bad habits. If there are too many people in a class, it is likely that the teacher won't be able to see their students and many things can go wrong. Students may argue amongst themselves because of uncertainty of the steps or moves or students try and teach other students which leads to the teacher having to correct and sometimes embarrass the student who decided to teach the others. All these pitfalls can be avoided by close observation of the students. You can ask the students to demonstrate their new moves in front of just yourself or in front of the whole class. The point of asking students to demonstrate in front of the whole class is not to embarrass them but to prepare them for social dancing. One of the biggest barriers for beginners is dancing in public. This barrier can only be broken down by gradually improving the students' confidence in a small arena of fellow students. Eventually the students will be confident enough to dance in front of anyone in public. Referring back to Maslow's Hierarchy of Needs the student must have a sense of belonging, then self esteem before they reach a level of self fulfilment. The teacher must develop the psychological approach of the student in addition to their dance skills. This leads to better development of the student.

Your Guide to Becoming a Qualified Salsa Teacher

REVIEW:

1 How many reasons are given for student wanting to do salsa?

2 How often do students need to practice salsa in order to improve?

3 How can you assess a student's salsa dance ability?

How to Make a Business Out Of Teaching

The ability to convert ideas into things is the secret of outward success.
Henry Ward Beecher 1813 Proverbs from Plymouth Pulpit 1887

The first thing to consider before anything else is to create a business plan.

This plan will cover everything from marketing, advertising, financial forecasts to venue hire and the overall budget. Here's a guide to a business plan:

1. About Yourself
2. Current business and Market Place
3. Competitor Analysis
4. Customer Profile
5. Target Market
6. Strengths, Weaknesses, Opportunities and Threats (S.W.O.T)
7. Your Vision for the Teaching Practice
8. Additional Information
9. Profit & Loss
10. Cash Flow Forecasts
11. Funding

12. Signing your plan

Current business

Describe the teaching practice, the condition it is in, its facilities and any relevant trading history. Discuss what the immediate area is like i.e. whether it is residential, local business, shops or rural.

Demographics

Describe the people that live, work and are in the immediate area. Think about their age, occupation, wealth and housing. It is important that you show a clear understanding of who is in the area i.e. who are your most likely customers.

Local Investment

Are there any changes due in the area such as investment projects i.e. community development? Is the area improving or declining?

Local Market Place

Where do people in the area spend their leisure time?

COMPETITION ANALYSIS

Name	What do they offer?	Who are their customers?	Could / Should you attract their customers

Your Guide to Becoming a Qualified Salsa Teacher

and if so how?

Customer Profile Existing

Who are the existing customers?

AM / Lunchtime

Mid afternoon/Early evening

Evening/Late

Target Market

Describe the customers you would like to attract.

S.W.O.T Analysis

Now that you have formed an idea of the teaching practice itself, the market place, current customers and potential customers it is useful for you to then identify areas of strengths and weaknesses within the business. This will help you to make the vital decisions to build your business and achieve maximum success.

Strengths

Identify all issues that are a positive benefit to the business.

Weaknesses
Identify all the issues that need addressing.

Your Guide to Becoming a Qualified Salsa Teacher

Opportunities

Describe what you think are the best opportunities within the business

Threats

Identify what you think are the risks to the business.

The Vision

Describe what you intend to do in order to attract custom. Mention specifically your intentions regarding dance styles taught, the structure of teaching, the venue, live music, entertainment, promotions and marketing. How will you accommodate smokers that visit the teaching practice? Earmark what is going to be special about what you are going to do to attract people to your teaching practice.

Additional Information

Is there any additional information you would like to add?

Include in this your cash flow forecast and your 12 month profit and loss forecast add to this a funding section and finish it off by signing it off and dating it. If you have a business manager you would add their name. Once you have done the above you will have a clear strategy for business as a salsa dance teacher.

The Venue

Where should you start teaching salsa? That will depend much on whether you are starting as a part-time or full time teacher. If you want to teach lots of technique and maintain your students' attention without distractions, a dance studio is the best place to start. If you are focusing on the social side of salsa teaching where there will be many a distractions but a more social environment, then a club, bar or restaurant would better suited.

 The location: from many stand points, you will have no business i.e. customers, if no one knows where you are based. You should look for a location which is preferably visible form a main road. The venue owner may allow you to put up a banner outside or large posters which will be visible to 1000's of people every day. This will create massive savings on your advertising budget.

Dance studio or nightclub, bar restaurant? If you are looking at a high turnover, and large numbers of customers then a nightclub/ bar would be most appropriate. This is the type of venue that is designed for social dancing.

The benefits of using a bar /night club venue:

You already have a captive audience who will already be using the bar. The bar manager will normally allow you to advertise outside the club. The bar manager normally assists in advertising your salsa class. This will save on your budget. The bar may even pay you the teacher to play music after the class and be their DJ for the night.

The disadvantages to using public bars and clubs:

The bar manager will advertise the class in their own way and design their adverts but this will not always give to true reflection of what you the teacher will be teaching. So if possible always design the advert yourself. Even professional designers have an often false concept of what salsa. If you cannot design the poster yourself make sure that you have seen it and checked it off before it goes to print. The success of your business depends on it.

When there are special sporting events the bar manager sometimes will cancel the salsa class with no notice. You will lose your customers for the night and possibly their loyalty because you didn't give them notice of the cancellation. Your customers may have travelled a long way to attend your class.

Bars and clubs don't have any assessment procedure so you will get people with no experience coming along and attending the intermediate or advanced class and totally disrupting the speed of teaching and learning. If students are at the wrong level, the teacher should make it clear to the student that they are not ready. This is important because if students deludes themselves that they are competent when they are not it will reflect on you as a teacher. A little bit of embarrassment might occur on the students' part but not as much embarrassment as if nobody wants to dance with them in the nightclub after the class.

Marketing:

How do we market a salsa class or workshop? We must go back to where we started and decided what styles of salsa we want to teach and what our teaching style is. When we have this concept crystallized we can sort out the marketing. You can find your potential market in many ways. Here are a few strategies:

Find out:

Who your competitors are and where they teach within a certain mile radius.

Is there a saturation of salsa teachers for the area or is there a demand for salsa with only one teacher in the area?

Is there a possibility of co-existence for salsa teachers where there is no conflict of classes on the same day? There is an assumption by many salsa clients/customers that salsa dancing is exempt from the rules of competition and that everyone on the salsa social scene are all friends because that's the nature of Latin dance. If you are of the same belief then you will be in for a big culture shock when you start to teach salsa. Many people who gladly greeted you with a friendly smile and handshake when you came to their club or dance school will ignore you or worse do their utmost to make sure you don't succeed in your salsa dance practice. After a few months it will sink in that salsa dance is exactly the same as any other leisure business. It has the appearance of excitement, fun and community but in reality everyone is practising their hospitality skills so that the customer comes back to their club and keeps their cash flow healthy.

The pit falls of competition:

Business can be extremely cut throat and caution should be used when sharing your business ideas. You could be telling a potential competitor who will take your idea and claim it for themselves.

Competitors who have a monopoly will actively seek to stop you from being successful. They will pull down your banners and posters, phone up potential customers and announce your event has been cancelled when they know it hasn't been; they will tell their students not to attend your classes, or tell them you are not experienced or competent enough to teach salsa. They will muddy your name with rumours and gossip, and even try to have your funding or capital withdrawn, almost anything to stop you succeeding. The hardest part about being a salsa teacher, is dealing with other salsa teachers - the criticism, the gossip and the rumour. If you can deal with these elements then you should have more than enough strength to succeed.

Advertising:

"Advertising is the most fun you can have with your clothes on"

Jerry Della Femina, US Advertising Exec.

Your Guide to Becoming a Qualified Salsa Teacher

Advertising is where the majority of your budget will go. Salsa is a dance which requires a lot of publicity and many classes have a high turnover of customers.

Advertising must go out every week. The most successful method of advertising is to have a banner or large A1 or A2 poster outside the venue stating the salsa class times, days and a contact number. This is the number one way to get people in your dance class. The exposure reaches thousands of people every day. If you did no other advertising this is the one that you must do. The second most successful way of advertising your class is by handing out flyers to everyone you meet - friends, family, shop assistants, and the cashier in the bank!

Another means of advertising which can accumulate clients quickly is internet advertising. If you have a website this will help build your client base very quickly by emailing past and present customers, and sending texts to interested parties. Emailing and texting must be done to interested parties who have signed up for the information, if they have not signed up for information, all you are doing is annoying your potential clients (spamming them) and wasting your money.

Finance:

Balance the budget with the limited finances you have. The Salsa class business has a very healthy turn over. The start up costs are very low for salsa teachers, all you need is room or venue hire which averages between £25 and £50 per hour in social clubs and fitness centres.

Bars generally are happy to offer free room hire on the assumption that students will buy refreshments from the bar. Students generally pay for their classes in cash unless they are paying for a course.

Colour posters in A1 size can be purchased for about £20. Flyers can be purchased at £90 per 5000 colour double sided gloss. To stay within budget never purchase advertising material from the city centre high street shop, they sometimes sell at three times the price you can get from urban shops or the internet. Considering the above, a class can be launched with two A1 posters= £40, a 5/2 foot banner =£50, 5000 flyers = £90 and room hire for eight weeks 8x£25 = £200. This totals £380. This cost can be recouped very quickly because there are very few running costs. However the teacher needs to pay for their teacher training exam = £210, yearly public liability insurances = £120, and First Aid certificate=£60. This cost totals £390. If you are teaching for schools or education establishments where the duty of care is higher because young and vulnerable people are taught, CRB check disclosure are needed at the of cost £45. Total start up costs of advertising £380 multiplied by six classes (6 X 8 weeks = 48) to cover one whole year= £2280 + Training and insurances £390 + CRB disclosures £45, = a total annual expense of £ 2715.

Legal requirements of tax,

The dance teacher must declare their earnings to the customs and excise which allows them to work out the dance teachers' income tax payments. The teacher should only be VAT registered if he or she earns above £67,000 for the previous twelve months of earnings. You are

Your Guide to Becoming a Qualified Salsa Teacher

advised to find an accountant to do your tax return otherwise you might spend more time sorting out your taxes than teaching dance.

Reference: www.hmrc.gov.uk

Chapter 5

In this chapter you learn about:

- what can happen during your first salsa class

- cases scenarios and questions

- a 10 point teacher checklist of what you will before you start teaching

- references sources for further study

Your Guide to Becoming a Qualified Salsa Teacher

"There are no great teachers only great pupils" Hans Von Bulow.

Case study practice exercises

Materials: You will need a pen and paper to write with.

Here is a list of scenarios that you may come across in your teaching
practice. Read the scenario and then write out your response to the
hypothetical situations.

Your first salsa class

You have decided to teach salsa dancing and you have done all your
advertising, hired the studio or bar. You have prepared your music and
what you intend to teach. Consider what you would do in each of the
following case scenarios.

1: Too many people arrive:

Over 60 people turn up and they are all eager beginners wanting to learn
how to salsa. However the room can only hold 40 people. The room is
crowded, what do you do?

A: Just continue and hope that no one gets injured.

B: Call your assistant and suspend the class until they arrive.

C: Split the class into 2 and arrange separate classes.

Possible approaches:

Your Guide to Becoming a Qualified Salsa Teacher

A is not advised because of injury risk. B will probably make students frustrated and they are likely to leave before your assistant arrives. Answer C would be the more sensible choice. Ensure that everyone has arrived for the beginners' class. It often happens that some people don't read the advertising properly and turn up at the wrong time. Not everyone might be there to take part in the class; some people may have just turned up for the intermediate class at a later time or to watch before deciding to come the next time you teach.

Explain that the room you have can only hold a certain number of people safely. Add that it would be for their benefit that you had a smaller group. You could split the group into 2 and offer to teach in half hour sessions if the class was supposed to be for 1 hour. Or find out if some people would be interested in returning in the following hour.

If you have an assistant, you could teach or ask that person to demonstrate the moves and steps in the warm up in another room and then you cover when more in depth technique or knowledge is required.

If there is a smaller room, you could induct the students and offer refreshments for them and maybe show some video clips of salsa dancing or demonstrate some of the products you may have for sale.

The final option is to turn people away but offer them some incentive to return and compensation for their wasted time such as a small discount on the next class or on some of your products.

Your Guide to Becoming a Qualified Salsa Teacher

If you decide to do the class with too many people it will result in a lot of complaints from people who will say they can't see or hear the teacher. Students don't understand and don't feel they have a chance to speak in a crowded room. Most importantly for the teacher there could be a health and safety risk in that there is a higher chance people will bump into each other or the fittings and fixtures of the room. The teacher will also not be able to observe and supervise the class properly. This will stop the teacher from doing their job properly. The end result is that less people will take the class because of their frustrations in not learning much.

2: Only 1 person arrives:
If only one person turns up to your first class and you have prepared to teach a large class, what do you do?

A: Become frustrated that you spent all the money on advertising and just cancel the class.
B: Continue with the class in a positive mood that you have your first ever customer.
C: Give the student the option of doing a private lesson.

Choice B is the answer more likely to gain long term rewards. C will only work if no one else turns up late, but people normally turn up a few minutes late in public classes. Only one person turning up is not uncommon in new salsa classes. Often people who intend to come simply forget to because the salsa class is not yet part of their routine. Sometimes students who intend to come to salsa don't do it for many weeks or even months. The teacher should not be put off or frustrated that only one person has arrived to take the class. Your focus should always be a professional one. If the student wants to learn and has travelled to do it then the least a teacher can do is respect the students effort in turning up. The student will be graced with a private lesson at the same price as a group lesson.

When proceeding with a lesson for one person might not prove fruitful. If the class is taking place in a public bar or night club, the student may feel self conscious of the public watching and the bar manager won't be happy because there won't be much income from sales of drink at their bar. Also if the teacher is paying for the room hire at e.g. £25 and the salsa class costs £5, the loss of £20 is probably not worth doing a lesson. However if this is a loss that the teacher can bear then the teacher should continue and consider the first class a loss leader. A loss leader is where it is accepted that in the first few weeks a loss will be made. Once the first month has passed and everyone who has taken the class has told their friends and work colleges, the teacher has a potential pool of hundreds of people who may have heard about the class by word of mouth. In business there is no better advertisement than word of mouth. It is your customer's testimony that you are providing a good service.

Difficult students' scenarios:

3: A student tries to teach other people in the class incorrectly or correctly.

A: Let them continue as they are helping you.

B: Tell them to leave the teaching to the teacher.
C: Tell them their help is appreciated but to ask for permission to demonstrate before doing so.

C is the correct answer. You shouldn't have someone unqualified and uninsured teaching without your permission. A is a common event in the classroom situation. If someone goes to the toilet or takes a phone call and misses five minutes of the class, other students will try and be helpful and show them what they have just missed. If the teacher is observant then this can be picked up. If, on the other hand, the student wants to show other students because they assume they know better than others then this raises a series of problems. Firstly, the student is assuming that the job of a teacher doesn't require any skill, and secondly, the student will be creating a portion of students doing things differently to what the teacher requires. The teacher will have to then retrain the other students. The approach: the student must be taken to one side and told that his or her help is appreciated but you are responsible for what is taught and how it is taught. Let them know that if anyone was injured in the class that you would be responsible and not them. This requires leadership from the teacher and the student should not be let off because if it continues, it won't be long before they think they can take over your class.

4: A student contradicts you the teacher.

A: Ask the student to leave the class.
B: Ask student where they got their information and compare with your source.

C: Ignore the student.

Both A and C should be avoided because they will cause repercussions in the future. Situation A will cause the student to despise you forever and situation C will allow the student to contradict you at a later stage and negatively affect the minds of other students. B is the best choice to make. It is possible to have a student who sometimes knows things that the teacher doesn't know, even in a beginners' class, if it relates to the history of the dance or musical interpretation. If the student claims to know more than the teacher in a beginners' class then this suggests the student is not a beginner. This student may have different motives for being in the class e.g. they want to socialise, meet a partner, is a teacher t and wants to check out the competition! Whatever the reason, the teacher must approach this situation with diplomacy and politeness. Ask where the student found this information and then tell the student your source of information and why you teach based on this source. If a student persists in contradicting and interrupting your class, there is not much point in them being there or you teaching them. You should refer the student to your ground rules for respect and participation. If the problem continues the student should be politely referred to a more appropriate class. Preferably not one of yours! Not all teachers are suitable for all students regardless of the subject matter some personalities find it hard to co-exist.

5: A student just doesn't get the moves:

A: Point and laugh at the student.
B: Assume the student is slow and just continue.

C: Give the student individual attention.

A is not to be done in any circumstances because it is unprofessional and will destroy the students confidence. Option B will only lead to a frustrated student who will not come back. C is the correct answer. There are many people who have problems with coordination and timing, this is not unusual. One of the key skills a teacher can have is patience. This skill can be used to find out why the student isn't learning. It could be the teachers fault; maybe explanations are not clear enough. The student may have a slight hearing or sight impairment or dyspraxia, a condition which affects the balance and coordination of the person. If they have dyspraxia the student will take perhaps two or three times longer to learn the steps and moves. This condition should be assessed at the very beginning with an initial assessment. All students should be asked about past injuries and medical conditions. It should be assessed from the beginning whether the class is appropriate for the student. Private lessons or special supervision of a helper may be required and should be factored into your teaching practice.

6: A student is drunk in a club or bar restaurant:
A: Let them carry on, they are just having fun.
B: Ask security to remove them.
C: Talk to them and find out more.

C is the answer and the way to deal with it professionally. This is a situation which surprisingly doesn't happen much. The majority of people who take a salsa class are sober, very alert and keen to learn. A very small percentage of people will drink alcohol to obtain some Dutch courage. If this is the case, it may have the effect of relaxing them and making them more sociable, it may also have the effect of making them rude, careless and negligent. If you smell strong alcohol on a students' breath, the student should be asked if they have had a drink and if so how much. If you think it is excessive, the student must be asked to leave the class. This is an uncomfortable situation for both the teacher and the student but for everyone's health and safety, it is necessary. Drunk people sometimes start fights and this is the worst thing you can have happen.

7: A Student is aggressive:

A: Let them carry on.
B: Ask security to remove them.
C: Talk to them and find out more.

Again, C is the answer and the way to deal with it professionally. If a student is aggressive, and doesn't seem to respect the other students, or you the teacher, ask the student if they are ok, and probe deeper into their behaviour it may be that they have a condition or had a family bereavement, until you ask you don't know. If the student is just generally aggressive you must refer them to the ground rules which your students should be made to sign when they first signed up for the salsa class. If you don't have a ground rules policy, it will create problems for any conflict resolution.

8: Students want to advance to higher levels but don't practice enough:

A: Let them advance to the next level.

B: Test them in an assessment.

C: Ask them how long they have been dancing.

B is the correct answer and the way to deal with it professionally. This is a situation that occurs often because salsa is a social dance and many people have very little time for socialising. They roll their social dancing, exercise and relaxation needs into one salsa night or one salsa class. This raises very high expectations and it is very difficult for the teacher to supply all of those needs. Most classes emphasize one or two of these elements but to attain all three of them would require careful planning. A teacher should have a lesson plan which breaks down what is taught in the class and also what exercises the students need to do in order to improve. If the students are only interested in socialising then you will not get much improvement from them unless they practise salsa two or three times a week.

9: A student is epileptic:

A: Let them carry on.

B: Ask them to leave the class.

C: Talk to them and find out what extra assistance they need.

All medical conditions should be revealed to the teacher in the initial assessment questionnaire. When you are aware that the student is epileptic you must have a diagnostic assessment of the degree of epilepsy. It may be necessary for the person to have individual support and their appropriate medication at hand. Teachers should be First Aid certified and know what to do when one of their students have accidents or fall ill.

10: The student has a back injury and asks if it is ok to take part in the class:

A: Let them join the class.
B: Ask them for a doctors' recommendation.
C: Tell them it is at their own risk.

B is the correct answer because you as a teacher are not qualified nor insured to give medical advice. It is for the student to assess their physical health and tell the teacher on the initial questionnaire. The teacher must then decide whether to allow the student in the class. If the student persists in asking for permission to join the class the teacher should deny them access. This action will involve strong leadership but will save the teacher from a potential personal injury claim.

11: A student is molesting other students:

A: Let them carry on!
B: Ask security to remove them.
C: Talk to them and find out more from both sides.

C is the answer before deciding on a course of action. You should have a ground rules agreement outlining what is acceptable behaviour and treatment for everyone in the class. We must refer back to the ground rules agreement that the student should sign at the very beginning of the class. If other participants are not being treated with respect, the student should be reminded of the breach. If it occurs again the student should be banned from the class. Lack of action from the teacher could be seen as silent consent to this abuse. Students have a high respect for teachers, this respect must not be bought into question because of the teachers' failure to observe and manage their class.

12: Your assistant teacher contradicts you:

A: Let them carry on.
B: Start an argument in front of the class.
C: Immediately talk to them in private and ask why.

C is the correct answer and will save the whole class a lot of embarrassment.   Your teaching practice may grow to the point where you need help to teach larger groups. You will need to hire some help. If you are hiring someone who is not qualified and therefore has not been verified by a national teaching body then the assistant will not know how to deal with many of the pit falls mentioned in this book. To ensure agreement with your assistant you must create a contract which should preferably be written although some people decide on verbal agreements and some people have no agreement whatsoever and deal with problems as they arise. Always have a written agreement. You should have a teaching lesson plan with the assistant and the assistant should be vetted because if they are not, and you just take their word that they have taught before, you are setting yourself up for serious problems in your class. If there is disagreement you should have a policy of how that is dealt with and it should not be aired or argued in front of the students.

If there is disagreement in front of students, they will assume that you don't respect each others' opinions and they may lose respect for you as a teacher. They may also assume that you are not a competent teacher.

13: Your assistant teacher attempts to poach your students:

A: Let them carry on.
B: Ask security to remove them!
C: Refer them to the non competition contractual agreement clause.

C is the correct answer. In most training contracts, the trainee wants to become independent and start their own teaching practice. If this is the case you must formulate a contract which restricts your assistant from taking the details of the business practice (your clients). A clause in the contract can also include restricting the assistants' work within a certain area from your base after they finish working with you. If you fail to ask the assistant to sign this agreement you leave yourself vulnerable to a takeover by your assistant. This happens in most fields of work, including salsa. If you don't have a contract with the assistant, there is nothing you can do to stop the assistant taking your hard earned clients. Salsa is a business and it must be executed in a business like way.

Your Guide to Becoming a Qualified Salsa Teacher

The Salsa Teacher 10 Point Checklist

1. Dance Teaching certificate, diploma, degree or QTS

A nationally accepted qualification is needed for city council employment.

2. First Aid certificate

The British Red Cross or St John's Ambulance offer all courses.

3. Teaching public liability insurance certificate

This should cover for over 1 million pounds.

4. Venue risk assessment forms

All venues should be inspected before use.

5. Child protection policy with reference to POCA /POVA acts

6. PPL and Royal Society music licences.

For all your music playing rights unless you have the copyright.

7. CRB Disclosures.

When working with children, young adults and vulnerable people.

8. Ground rules agreement.

Ensure it covers legal duties on equal opportunities.

9. Assistants and teachers standard form contracts

Include their rights as well as their responsibilities.

10. Teaching lesson plans.

Include plans for mixed ability, beginners, improvers, intermediate, and advanced.

Your Guide to Becoming a Qualified Salsa Teacher

Have the courage to follow your dreams.

"whatever you do you need courage; whatever you decide upon someone will always tell you that you're wrong. You will begin to doubt yourself and think that your critics are right. To have a plan and to follow it takes the courage of a lion." Ralph Waldo Emerson,

My dream is to see salsa dancing raised to a level where it can be appreciated by everyone of all races and social backgrounds; where it can be used to help people find how much they have in common with each other, rather than how different they are regardless of who they are or where they're from. Salsa is rich in culture because historically it connects us all to our roots. Salsa is a positive activity because it allows you the opportunity to feel spiritually uplifted, socially engaged and physically excited by its wonderful rhythms. Salsa is a gift that should be respected and shared by everyone.

The future of salsa dance.
Salsa dance will continue to grow as the Latin American continent develops. When globalisation of Latin American culture reaches full saturation there will be a great demand for qualified, responsible salsa teachers to raise this social dance to a respected art form.

To help you establish a base of salsa music, following is a list of the most influential artists and groups in the roots of salsa:

Musicians from Cuba: Antonio Arcano from Las Maravillas del Siglo, Israel and Orestes Lopez, Mario Baza, Machito and the Afro Cubans,

Orquestra America and Enrique Jorrin, Perez Prado, Orquesta Aragon, Antoni Machin and his hit, El Manicero), Arsenio Rodrigues, The Buena Vista Social Club (Cuban Super group of Cuban soneros), Omara Portuondo, Beny More and Celia Cruz, Sierra Maestra, Cubanismo, Early modern influential artists: Irakere, Los Van Van, NG La Banda, Isaac Delgado, Paulito y su elite, Manolin el medico dela salsa, Juan Carlos Alfonso y Dan Den, David Calzado y la Charanga Habanera,Candido Fabre, Jovenes Clasicos del son.
Other pioneers: Pablo Arminan (son, trova) Chano Pozo, Patata Valdes, Mongo Santa Maria.
From Colombia: Fruco y sus tesos, Joe Arroyo, Grupo Niche
From New York: Hector Lavoe, Ray Barretto, Victor Manuelle, Super groups: Fania All Stars, Spanish Harlem Orchestra. Alberto Socarras, Willie Colon Eddie and Eddie Palmieri, Ray Barretto. Tito Puente.
From Puerto Rico: Puerto Rican Power, El Gran Combo, Sonora Poncena, Ismael Rivera.
Dancers: From Cuba: Orestes Lopez, From Puerto Rico: Cuban Pete,

From New York: Eddie Torres, from Los Angeles: Edie the Salsa Freak,

From Mexico: The Vasquez Brother: Luis, Fransisco and Johnny

Vasquez.

References

Legislation:
Copyright, Designs and Patents Act 1988
Children Act 2004

Your Guide to Becoming a Qualified Salsa Teacher

Licensing Act 2003

Race Relations Act 1976,

The Sex Discrimination Act 1975

Human Rights Act.

The Disability Discrimination Act 1995

Data Protection Act 1998

Health and Safety at Work Act 1974

Discograpghy: Salsa CDs.

El Barbaro del ritmo: Mambos by Beny More; Tumbao Cuban Classics.

La coleccion cubana, Omara Portuondo,

Master cuts Latin Jazz.

Salsa Dance, the Rough Guide,

The Very Best Of Salsa, Nascente,

The Beginners Guide To Salsa, Nascente.

The Beginners Guide To Cuba. Nascente.

The Essential Guide To Salsa, Union Square Music Ltd.

Videography: DVD and VHS.

Buena Vista Social Club. Film 4. (1999)

Cuba Rhythms unpacked: A unique exploration of Cuba's most famous musical styles.

Son Sabroson Antesala de la Salsa, Documental historico, serie vengo de cuba. (1999)

Salsa, A Jeremey Marre Documentary Harcourt Fimls (1979).

Salsa a la Cubana. Eric Freeman Productions

Salsa night club style: New York Style with Eddie Torres. (1996) VHS.

The Roots of Rhythm with Harry Belafonte. (1994)

Your Guide to Becoming a Qualified Salsa Teacher

Absolute Beginners Salsa, Spirit Salsa 2006
Intermediate Salsa Spirit Salsa 2007.

Internet website references and sources:
www.spiritsalsa.com Salsa teacher training workshops based in the UK.
www.Descarga.com/cgi-bin/db/archives/Article17 .
www.Wikipedia.com
www.Yahoo.videos.com
http://uk.youtube.com/user/spiritsalsa
www.salsapower.com
www.salsa-merengue.co.uk
http://www.teachpe.com/anatomy/muscles.php
www.artscouncil.org.uk
http://www.opsi.gov.uk/Acts/acts1991/ukpga_19910048_en_1

Bibliography
A Reference Manual For Teachers Of Dance Exercise. J May Et Al (W.
Foulshham & Co Ltd. 1998
Antons Dance Class By Anton Dubeke, London 2007.
British Dance Council Rule Book 2005
Caribbean Dance From Abakua To Zouk. Sloat, Susanna, University
Press Of Florida 2005
History and the Morris Dance, John |Cutting, Dance Books, Hampshire,
2005
Learn To Dance Modern Jive. R Austin – C Hilliard 1998.
Jazz Latino, Isabelle Leymarie, Cuba, Brasil, Y Sudamerica En El Jazz.
Manon Tropo 2003.

Play Congas Now The Basics And Beyond.Richie Gajate-Garcia) Sigma-Cheshire Warner 2000.

Santeria From Africa To The New World. The Dead Sell Memories By George Brandon. Indian University Press 1997.

Salsa- The Musical Heart Beat Of Latin America- Sue Steward. Thomas-Hadson London 1999.

Sobrevivir En El Baile Latino. Javier Garcia Egocheaga Et Al Tikal Ediciones (Madrid).

The Garland Handbook of Latin American Music, 2nd ed, Dale A, Olsen and Daniel El. Sheehny. Routledge New York, 2008

The World Of African Music By Ronnie Graham Pluto, 1992.

The Rough Guide To Cuban Music Philipe Sweeney 2001.

The Rough Guide To The Caribbean Oct 2002.

The English Dancing Master, John Playford.

UKA 2005 Year Book

Your Guide to Becoming a Qualified Salsa Teacher

Salsa Teachers
Guide Book

Your Guide To Becoming A Qualified Salsa Teacher:

Salsa dancing is a massively expanding industry in the UK and the world. The development of Latin America and the Caribbean has lead to increased interest in salsa classes and Latin music. New salsa moves and styles are regularly being introduced, but how do you become a salsa teacher? "Your Guide To Becoming A Qualified Salsa Teacher" will provide the answers and an insight into this exciting social art form. It also includes a 20 week training syllabus of salsa moves from Cuba, New York, Los Angeles and Colombia so that you too can learn how to qualify as a salsa teacher. For information email: info@spiritsalsa.com

ISBN 978-0-9532429-2-4

9 780953 242924

www.spiritsalsa.com